On the Cusp of a Dangerous Year

Crab Orchard Series in Poetry
Editor's Selection

On the Cusp of a Dangerous Year

LEE ANN RORIPAUGH

Crab Orchard Review

&

Southern Illinois University Press

CARBONDALE

24 23 22 21   7 6 5 4

The Crab Orchard Series in Poetry is a joint publishing
venture of Southern Illinois University Press and *Crab
Orchard Review.* This series has been made possible by the
generous support of the Office of the President of Southern
Illinois University and the Office of the Vice Chancellor
for Academic Affairs and Provost at Southern Illinois
University Carbondale.

Crab Orchard Series in Poetry Editor: Jon Tribble

Library of Congress Cataloging-in-Publication Data
Roripaugh, Lee Ann.
  On the cusp of a dangerous year / Lee Ann Roripaugh.
    p. cm. — (Crab Orchard series in poetry)
  ISBN-13: 978-0-8093-2929-8 (alk. paper)
  ISBN-10: 0-8093-2929-8 (alk. paper)
  I. Title.
  PS3568.O717O5 2009
  811'.54—dc22   2009007805

One day Lord Korechika, the Minister of the Centre, brought the Empress a bundle of notebooks. "What shall we do with them?" Her Majesty asked me. "The Emperor has already made arrangements for copying the *Records of the Historian*."

"Let me make them into a pillow," I said.

"Very well," said Her Majesty. "You may have them."

I now had a vast quantity of paper at my disposal, and I set about filling the notebooks with odd facts, stories from the past, and all sorts of other things, often including the most trivial material. On the whole I concentrated on things and people that I found charming and splendid; my notes are also full of poems and observations on trees and plants, birds and insects.

— Sei Shonagon (c. 965 to after 1010), *The Pillow Book*

Seeing the water birds on the lake increase in number day by day, I thought to myself how nice it would be if it snowed before we got back to the Palace—the garden would look so beautiful; and then, two days later, while I was away on a short visit, lo and behold, it did snow. As I watched the rather drab scene at home, I felt both depressed and confused. For some years now I had existed from day to day in listless fashion, taking note of the flowers, the birds in song, the way the skies change from season to season, the moon, the frost and snow, doing little more than registering the passage of time. How would it all turn out?

— Murasaki Shikibu (c. 973 to 1014 or 1025), *The Diary of Lady Murasaki*

Contents

Acknowledgments

Poems in this book or excerpts have appeared or are
forthcoming in the following journals:

> *Alaska Quarterly Review*—"Crows Who Try to Be Cormorants Drown"
>
> *Beloit Poetry Journal*—"Things I Would Do for You"
>
> *BLOOM*—"Insect Postures"
>
> *coconut*—"Chambered Nautilus," "The Desire for Space Travel Is a Metaphor for Escape," and "Marvelous Things"
>
> *Crab Orchard Review*—"Luscious Things"
>
> *Cream City Review*—"Things That Cause a Feeling of Chagrin"
>
> *diode*—"Hegemony, Anemone, Chalcedony, Persephone" and "Things That Are Filled with Grace"
>
> *Mid-American Review*—"Temporary Things"
>
> *Mipoesias*—"Disconcerting Things," "Salty Things," "Squalid Things," "Ukiyo: The Floating World," and "Utsuroi"
>
> *North American Review*—"Notes on the Cusp of a Dangerous Year"
>
> *Puerto del Sol*—"Disconsolate Things"
>
> *Shenandoah*—"Bioluminescence"
>
> *Southern Review*—"Cecropia" and "Objects in the Mirror"

"Bioluminescence" was reprinted in *Digerati*, edited by Steve Mueske, Three Candles Press, 2006.

"Snow Country" was published in *Under the Rock Umbrella: Contemporary American Poets from 1951–1977*, edited by William Walsh, Mercer University Press, 2006.

The author would also like to gratefully acknowledge grants received from the Archibald Bush Foundation and the South Dakota Arts Council.

1

season of

the

dog day

cicadas

Crows Who Try to Be Cormorants Drown

7:00 A.M., and in the crepuscular gray-silk light
shimmering pairs of raised socket rings rimming
the eyes of goldfish glint like burnished mother-
of-pearl. Their shadowed bodies have the bored,
languorous air of fan dancers French-inhaling
Lucky Strikes backstage before the dusty velvet
curtain creaks, then comes clattering up. Peach
green tea dallies in my mouth like a nostalgia
of fat, silky petals, and the Siamese cat rests
one chill, suspiciously damp paw on my neck.
The scent of sunburnt peaches arabesques in a fine
wraith of steam from the blue mug the way your
name kept twizzling, curlicuing and disappearing
through my sleep last night, slippery between
my fingers, smooth and fine as cinnamon.

I think of Elizabeth Bishop in Brazil and how,
in her letters to friends, she kept exclaiming,
The snails here are as big as dinner plates!
Did you know snails are hermaphrodites?
Or that, during courtship, they slowly circle one
another, lightly touching each other along the neck
with their antennae-tipped eyes and nudging
their soft, blunt heads, forehead to forehead, before
firing off a pair of fierce love darts, to break
each other's skin and pierce the tender flesh inside?
Isn't it a strange thought? A love dart?
But really, aren't we all strange fruit ripening
outward from our navels—dusky or pale, fleshy
and moonstruck—after being clipped from the vine?
And don't we cushion our hearts like big cracked
seeds inside a tangled nest of membrane, skin

and pulp before they whirl away like dervishes
on propeller-light wings, or end up tucked into
the dark musky cheeks of squirrels, when the body's
false promises have long been forgotten?

Although maybe that's not true. Maybe our hearts
aren't seeds, but birds. Maybe our hearts
are cormorants, diving at night for sweet fish
in a blaze of torch light on the Nagara River
in Japan, and our bodies are the leather rings
fishermen strap around the necks of the birds
to keep them from swallowing the fish. And still
mine keeps diving, diving through the night,
against a bone-hollowing hunger unfulfilled,
and even in spite of the old Japanese folk saying:
Crows who try to be cormorants drown.

My tea cools, morning grips the sun between
thumb and forefinger like a lemonade corkscrew
Akro Agate Popeye marble shooter. Outside
the windowpane, a wasp, arms and legs akimbo,
cleans her satin-banded body with the same
seductive gesture as a woman smoothing down
a cocktail dress over the swell of her hips.
And I circle around this poem too many times,
awkward even in the inching tarantellas of mollusk
love. But soon, soon I will find the words
that pierce clean through, and soon I will find
their center—like a slice of silver splitting
the air in a smoke-filled room. For the mean-
time, though, did you know, my love,
that a flock of larks is called an *exaltation*?

Disconsolate Things

The dull dusted thud of powdery moths,
somewhat like the weight

of a fat summer raindrop, striking their
plump, furred bodies up

against a lit windowpane—the muffled
sound, a strangled

rupture, like hot bright kernels of popcorn,
incandescent,

blooming into stark white clouds. The liquid
and silent slip

of a garter snake startled while dozing
on my porch step's

sun-baked stone—its fluorescent yellow stripes,
warmly oiled scales,

disappearing into the chilly, rain-
drenched underbrush

of an ivied garden overtaken
with weeds, where one

remaining cricket chirps resolutely
into the night

like an obsessive-compulsive's weird reed
flute. A robin's egg

cracked open on the sidewalk, a broken
sky-blue gumball—

deep inside the fractured sun of gold yolk
a small black grape

seed of something, like the compactly furled
body of a

mosquito floating in amber. Soon ants
come in matter-

of-fact regiments to ravenously
sip albumen

from shards now paling in heat to turquoise,
pausing between

sips to clean, with a fussy precision,
the stickiness

of their antennae with even stickier
feet. And down from

the porch overhang, a fat orb-weaver
spider, purplish-

blue, lets down her drag line to hang and bob,
legs tickling silk

like a flamenco guitarist plucking
repeated-note

patterns on a single string. Seeing me,
with myopic

bulging eyes, she pauses, then curls herself
into a tight

round ball and dangles like an overripe
blueberry. Late

summer grasshoppers, a pair of them, grip
the window screens

with their dainty tenterhook feet, legs coiled
like mighty jack-

in-the-box springs, basking and spitting in
the easy give

and take of their weeklong camaraderie.
And when night comes,

the wind will touch me with long, cool, supple
fingers, and in

another house somewhere, a woman will
unbraid the soft

red plaits of another woman's hair, brush
it out until

wiry strands crackle with a life all their own
and her hands fill

with electricity—a spark against
the wrist, the warm

profusion of scalp musk, a flickering
bouquet of flame-

bright poppies, embered and luminous, and
hungry for air.

Notes on the Cusp of a Dangerous Year

Thirty-seven, the year Lady Murasaki called
the dangerous year, approaching. . . .

Today, a cold drizzle of rain trickles down
in soft, plangent icy drops seeping low
into the bones. The tree in the front yard,
whose leaves turned bright lime green
and phosphorescent yellow, shimmers wetly,
branches weighted with damp. A squirrel,
fur in moist spikes along his back, complains
at me from his perch with chuttering
coughs and whips his tail in frenetic
aggressive circles like plumed numchucks.

Cats mashed in a warm pile on the futon—
the season of heat-leeching begun. Earlier
in the morning, each cat flung across the bed
like a discarded sock, toasted below by the quiet,
patient ticking of the electric blanket:
pleasured swoon, opiate warmth, eyes slitted
half open, and limbs melting to pliable
honey. When I poked at them, they only
emitted sullen grunts of acquiescence.

I should wash the dishes, step shiveringly
into the cold drafty porcelain of the shower.
I should water plants, grade papers, separate
light from dark, delicate from indelicate,
I should, I should, I should . . .

Everywhere there are ladybugs—clinging
to curtains, inching across linoleum, hunched
incongruously on the handle of the Mr. Coffee

carafe, a row of them gripping the laptop's
electrical cord. There is something oddly *fluid*
in the way they unspool their paths—legs
pumping and scurrying below in a jerky,
mechanical synchronicity, while from above
all one sees are the polished domes of orange
and black-spotted armors serenely rolling
forward across the floor. When I pick them up,
they seem like perfectly halved glittering
lacquerware beans. The other day I found a pair—
one sixteen-spotted and bright yellow, the other
a blank, deep rust—sexing each other up,
flagrante delicto, on the arm of my Adirondack
chair on the front porch. Afterwards, the rust one
split open the candy-shell coating of its back
(smooth, Lamborghini-like hydraulics of upraised
elytra, shocking glimpse of delicate, black-tissue-
paper wings unfurling underneath) and flew away.

The moths who come at night are darker—sooty
black or charcoal-grey—bodies and wings stockier,
more heavily furred, as if they were bundled
in ermine. I find I am lonesome for the evanescent
visitations of my summer insects: the glitter-eyed
violet dragonflies; clumsy bumbling rattle of cicadas
striking the windowpane; and the space-alien katy-
dids, with their wings like two fresh bay leaves.

Tonight, a smoky roll of gray-black marbled clouds
obscures the stars—the clouds backlit by a hot, yellow
spotlight of a moon, giving a creamy and feverish
butter-colored cast to their tender underbellies
and wispy nebulaed edges as they slide across the sky.
If you're a coldly twisting mass of cloud on the lam,
does it mean you can get burnt by the moon?

Shortly after midnight, I find a present of pumpkins
outside my door. A tall, left-leaning skinny pumpkin,
and a round squat one splashed and mottled in
zucchini greens. Mysterious, anonymously gifted
pumpkins. Did someone know that it's my birthday?
Did they have any idea how much the solid heft,
the dusty orange creases, this quintessential
pumpkin-ness fills me with intense pleasure?

It's chilly, quiet—solitude broken only by words
beginning to obsessively circle the duplicitous sphere
of the porch light like ghosts of summer insects:
Ephemera, Lamentation, Samovar, Willow.
One by one, I capture them, strike them each
like matches, and cup their soft blaze in my hands.
I feel their candled glow, flickering yellow heat,
for just one moment . . . and then I blow them out.

Squalid Things

A long glossy line of fat ants who've squeezed
themselves under

the back-door crack, clambering up into
the bowls of cat

food to wallow about, all the while ges-
ticulating

imperiously with their antennae.
The cats look down

in their food bowls and refuse to eat, then
look up at me

in shock and disgust. A fly who's been trapped
in the sticky

gum of flypaper—struggling, contorting
itself into

the twisted poses of a Mannerist
painting, or as

if it were playing a game of Twister,
buzzing so loud

it becomes impossible to ignore
the horribleness

of its predicament, until one starts
to feel stricken

with remorse, but can't think of any way
to rectify

the situation other than to hum,
at top volume,

the tune to the Alka Seltzer jingle
just to drown out

the death rattle until, at last, it stops.
Needless to say,

this is very squalid. The crisp Texas
okra pickles

that one sometimes likes to eat in secret
are really quite

squalid too, as their green skins are ever-
so-slightly, most-

disturbingly furred, just like the tender
flesh of earlobes.

The ex-girlfriend who incessantly made
comparisons

to her former lovers: so-and-so's breasts
were more floppy,

or that it took at least four whole fingers
to fill so-and-

so's vagina, was hopelessly squalid.
When one's toilet

overflows it is so depressingly
squalid that one

simply wishes to move to a whole new
apartment. And

eating Lime Green Tostitos in bed while
swilling Rolling

Rock and reading books of questionable
literary

merit is squalid as well, even though
one can't always

help oneself. Also, a cat who will eat
another cat's

vomit, thinking it a form of soft food,
and hence a treat,

is a very squalid cat indeed. And
finally, when

one has been looking forward to having
dinner with one's

lover at an elegant restaurant,
but once there, she

starts to pick a fight while one is maybe
daydreaming a

little, and perhaps imagining that
one is Jean Rhys

in Paris about to order absinthe;
imagining

the waiter discreetly arrives with news-
paper sheathing

the decanter, brilliant emerald green
splashing over

the pristine snow-white sugar cube nestled
in the curve of

the metal spoon . . . and one's lover is now
becoming quite

angry and says she thinks she's still in love
with her ex-girl-

friend, and one notices that the waitstaff
are all starting

to smirk—well, this is perhaps the most
squalid thing of all.

Objects in the Mirror

I'm tired of being like the bee who's duped into mating
with *Ophrys* orchids mimicking winsome
female bees, only to discover a bee's not a bee,

and I'm nothing more than a glorified pollinator.
Isn't it better to be an insect
who pretends to be a flower, like the delicate-petaled

Malaysian orchid mantis, who entices crickets, flies,
locusts, and moths into her pink embrace?
(Ambuscade of bewildering mandibles, necks severed

in a single, guillotine-like strike. Such fierce clarity.)
Or how about the complex stratagems
of the *Maculinea* butterfly, who lays her eggs

inside wild buds of thyme? Her caterpillars hatch, eating
their way out of thyme until they become
steeped in it, sweating a spicy milk crazy-delicious

to red ants who, in a gluttonous haze, carry the soft
fragrant sultans back to the nest to be
bathed and groomed by worker ants. Then, like con-men in a heist

movie locked in the bank vault at night, the caterpillars
eat the stored hoard of ant larvae and eggs
before fleeing the scene of the crime in a sly disguise.

Or consider female Photuris fireflies, who copy
the intricate mating signal flashes
of other firefly species—the same way child prodigies

can play back, note for perfect note, an entire sonata
after no more than a single hearing—
in a performance so authentically compelling that

male fireflies respond to the coded flashing come-ons
as if they were one of their own, only
to be killed and consumed. Nothing really is as it seems,

and no one's really who or what they say they are. Hawk moth
caterpillars pass themselves off as snakes,
while deliciously edible Viceroy butterflies robe

themselves to look like toxic Monarchs, whose stained-glass orange
wings are spiked and window-paned with poison
Milkweed leaves. Everything's masquerade, subterfuge, and soap

opera, revealing only that it's arrogance to think
we could ever really know exactly
what it is we're getting into. Imagine tropical

male ants who chemically disguise themselves in the sultry
perfume of virgin queens—slipping past more
aggressive males to insinuate themselves into the quick

pulsing heart of the nest where, cross-dressed in female scent,
they, with their gentler art, are allowed to mate
with the queen. Please, just think of that should you ever find my

owlish decoy eye-spots unconvincing enough to wish
to tear into my wings. Take a moment
to think of that before you shame me for my illusions.

Luscious Things

1. Tangelo

The delicate spray of zest that spritzes
out when your finger-

nail first catches under the skin—pulling
it back to expose

the cool spicy fruit. Slipping a finger
under the membraned

sections to make then blossom out and yield
their seeds, their lacy

fretwork of pulp, the tangy-sweet spurt of
juice against the tongue.

2. Peach

A peach is more delicious when you take
the time to inhale

its fragrance first, rub your cheek up against
the tender furred curve

of its skin, lightly run your tongue along
the cleft, break the skin

with your teeth and press your mouth deep into
creamy golden flesh—

ravishing it bare right down to the bone
of red pitted stone.

3. Banana

Bananas are many things, but luscious?
Maybe not so much.

4. Fig

The fig enjoys a rather lusciously
perverted sex life,

with secret, ingrown flowers that never
see daylight sprouting

inside. Some figs are edible, others
house fig wasps who hatch

and mate. The male dies, while the female bursts
from the eye as if

reborn—honeyed with pollen, seeking more
ingrown flowers in

which to lay her eggs. She pierces fig eyes
to gain entrance, then

wriggles down the long, slender necks to find
those secret bloomings,

pollinating all she touches with her
wings, her mouth, her feet.

When you eat a fig you eat these secrets,
this pollen, her touch.

5. *Pomegranate*

It's thought that Eve might have been tempted by
the pomegranate

as opposed to the more quotidian
apple and really,

while apples are nice, they don't seem very
luscious to me . . . think

of the pomegranate's flowered calyx,
her jeweled ruby seeds

nestled in plush, egg-carton dimples of
membrane. Who wouldn't?

6. *Artichoke*

A thistle, yes, which might not seem luscious
at first, but there is

the scraping off of nutty flesh that's tugged
between the teeth—

base to tender tip. There's the way thistle
down scents the fingers

still hours later, the yielding creaminess
of heart melting against

tongue. Eat the bud, and let the bright violet
flower bloom inside.

2

during the

aftermath

of an

escaped moon

Hegemony, Anemone, Chalcedony, Persephone

All last week, trees simultaneously released
entire branchfuls of leaves with exasperated sighs.
They came clattering down like breakfast cereal.
How does it feel, I wonder, to relinquish oneself
to winter in this way? And is it the trees who cast off
their leaves, or do the leaves simply decide to let go?

Now, the first snowfall of the year. Dry, crisp flakes
seasoning down from the sky like many salt shakers
rhythmically shaken over the Missouri River Valley.
There's a sound like a rustling of taffeta skirts,
a shivery dusting of white coating sidewalks and lawns,
the hoods and roofs of cars. Like confectioner's sugar,
except for the blue undertone of *sparkle* thumbtacked
in steely points underneath the haloes of streetlamps,
showering flinty sparks in the headlights of passing cars.

I discover a remnant of summer, a dog day cicada,
in the mop bucket: army-tank greens and blacks
immaculately preserved, glittering fretwork of wings,
two hind legs raised akimbo, frozen mid-stride.
Was it one of the same cicadas who came in August
to dementedly orbit my porch light like the metal cars
in a Tilt-A-Whirl ride from a small-town parking lot
carnival? (Stung rain of clear metallic plinks ringing
against my windows.) Some landed on their backs
and couldn't right themselves, violently scraping
and buzzing, a rattling clamor of wings, like berserk
mechanical toys. I'd find ribbed husks shucked
in the foliage, neat slits down the back like discarded
peel-and-eat shrimp shells—exact cast likenesses down
to the slender pincer feet and bulging, wide-set eyes.

It's the time of year I'm drawn to pomegranates
at the grocery store: so private, so mysteriously
self-contained, with their lovely flowered crowns,
glittering garnet-colored seeds hidden inside
fleshy smiling dimples of pulp. I wish I had
an entire basket. I would stand on the sidewalk
in the snow, press them into the open palms
of beautiful women, saying *remember . . . ?*

It's a good night to drink large steaming mugs
of pungent ginger tea, to eat hot and sour soup
and black pepper chicken. A good night to wear
a Laplandish type of hat, with flappy ear flaps,
dangling pom-poms, and a soft fleece lining.
It's a good night to daydream over the dictionary,
turning over the deliciously thin pages one by one—
soft rustle of turning paper not unlike the sound
of snow outside—turning over the gently falling
sounds of the words in one's mouth like cold, round
sweet grapes: *hegemony, anemone, chalcedony,
Persephone.* And later, in the dark, it will be a good
night to dream one's lover has returned: to pull her
into the spooned curve of one's body, finger
the delicate ridge of her navel, smell the wispy hairs
at the nape of her neck, whisper secrets in her ear:
Did you know . . . ? I wish . . . And then . . .

Salty Things

The *ume-boshi* salt plum heart of rice
balls wrapped in seaweed,

their ripe-fruit texture a tart electric
shock on a tongue lulled

into complacency by the mildness
of sticky white grains.

A jar of pickled ginger opening
with a crusty rasp

caused by salt crystallizing in the grooved
threads for twisting on

the lid. Inside: red shredded ginger dyed
bright as Valentines

by *shoga* leaves, a burning tang of brine
and sharp spicy root.

There's no such thing as too many pickles:
the crunchy pungent

mustard-colored *takuan* pickles made from
daikon radishes

fermented in rice bran; plush aubergines
and crisp cucumbers,

called *shiba zuke*, magenta-colored
from having been steeped

in plum vinegar; the potent, boozy-
breathed cucumbers that

my mother always called *stink-o* pickles
because they were drunk—

literally pickled in rice wine mash—
or maybe *stink-o*

because they'd make you tipsy if you ate
too many too fast;

the fresh zest of homemade *nuka zuke*—
pickles marinated

in a crock of rice bran, tended daily
with offerings of

eggshells, rinds, beer, and wine—starter batches
passed down as heirlooms

from mother to daughter to remember
what home tastes like; or

natto, fermented soy beans, suspended
in redolent strands,

seasoned with soy sauce, biting hot mustard,
and beaten into

a sticky froth to eat over steaming bowls
of rice with names like

Kokuho Rose, Nishiki, Tsuru Mai
(the "flying stork" brand)

or Niko Niko (the "sound of smiling"
rice). And even then,

my hunger for salt unappeased, I'd wait
until my parents

left for Safeway or Albertsons to raid
their Frigidaire for

contraband pickles eaten on the sly
straight from the jar, my

fingertips puckering in sticky brine,
a flavor made more

delicious because it was illicit.
Even now, this taste

still a yearning I carry in my mouth:
a lust for salt, for

cool pale *daikon*, sour fragrant plums, rising
up to meet my tongue.

Insect Postures

If I could, I would have stopped myself, like the ladybug,
from being consumed, by leaking pungent,
bitter tears from my knee joints; or coated my body in

a whispered sheen of oil, like the cockroach, so I could
have slit myself between a paper-thin crack
and simply disappeared. If I could have eaten the leaves

of passionflower vines to make myself toxic, sprouting
fierce prickly spines and neon-yellow skin
so I could slumber in the shade like the postman butterfly's

caterpillar—filtering light and dark with a semi-
colon of six eyes punctuating each
side of my head—I would have. Perhaps if I had super

powers, and could leap sixty-five times my own height, flea-like,
to the top of the Empire State Building
in one bound, faster than a space rocket; or if I had

the strength of a rhinoceros beetle and could bench-press
850 times my own weight;
or maybe even with the housefly's less-pretentious-yet-

uncanny ability to taste with my hands and feet,
I could have rescued myself in the nick
of time. Maybe, if I were royalty, I would have been

declared exempt, spent my days like the queen wasp, nestling eggs
one at a time into their six-sided
paper cells, like snugging truffles into crinkly, gold-foil

accordion wrappers in a fine box of chocolates.
I wish I'd found some way to escape—
stowed away in a hummingbird nostril like the tiny

flower mite, riding from bloom to bloom as if they were bus
stops, hoping to finally arrive at
a more desirable flower on which to disembark.

If only I had ears on the sides of my abdomen
with which to hear the sonar of hunting
bats, so that like the moth, I could simply clasp my wings shut

and fall—a tight quiet triangle plummeting down from
the sky, no longer a blip on the radar,
light as a small paper note folded around the word *No*.

Disconcerting Things

It is highly disconcerting when the plumbing
in one's apartment, which is old and peevish,
ominously gurgles and clunks, when soapy water,
frilled bits of lettuce, burble up in one's sink
each time the neighbor washes his dishes,
and the bathtub drain thumps and glugs
throughout the basement washer's spin cycle.

When one finds a burnished, jet-black spider,
red triangle notched into its back, basking
in the sun on the kitchen windowsill, it's
unnervingly disconcerting since one can't
remember if black widows are branded
on their *bellies* or their *backs*. There's no time
to Google, so one gingerly slides an envelope
under the spider—making it flail about in a spry,
unpredictable fashion as one hustles it out
into the foliage with a distinct sense of unease.

Of course, neglecting to take one's Wellbutrin
is bound to produce disconcerting results.

It's also disconcertingly ghastly when an ex
comes pounding on the door, unannounced
and uninvited, declaring she's realized
her relationship problems have all been caused
by sleeping with people she's not attracted to . . .
meanwhile suggesting one might nonetheless
like to get it on with her while she's in town.
And it's not just the epiphany that she's even *more*
unbearable than one had made her out to be
to all one's friends, it's that the relationship,

however short-lived, insists on retaining
an infinite shelf life as a source of lingering
personal humiliation. *D'oh!* one wants to yelp,
smacking self in forehead as if auditioning
for a V-8 commercial. *What was I thinking?!*
one wants to shriek into the cold night air.

Does it go without saying that it's both
upsetting and disconcerting when the head
of one's favorite mounted yellow stag beetle
(*Odontolabis femoralis*) randomly falls off
and has to be glued back on with Super Glue?

Even an octopus can become severely disconcerted,
breaking off one of its own arms as a decoy
to predators so it can brood in uninterrupted solitude.
Meanwhile, the lone severed arm keeps changing
colors—chromatophores strobing like the throb
of disco lights—continuing to crawl, flop, twitch,
and dance in time to its own muscular backbeat
with a choreographed nonchalance, as if to suggest
that everything was fine . . . just fine.

The Desire for Space Travel Is a Metaphor for Escape

Christmas Eve, and how deliciously soft-shell crab
crackled in my mouth at the San Francisco sushi joint
where dishes circled on a mechanical conveyor belt
like a school of Cubist fish—price determined by size,
color, and shape of plate, customers lunging up to strike
at what looked tasty. I missed you, so I tried to remember
the delicate grit of breading, shell melting in a brittle
sizzle and flake against the teeth like phyllo pastry,
vinegary tang of Ponzu sauce, then the tender-
bellied flesh of stomach crumbling across my tongue
in a gray, sweet creamy paste. I wanted to tell you how,
stepping outside afterwards, the cool astringent pepper
of eucalyptus scoured the silvery night air into a high,
bright polish, how Christmas lights twittered in palm trees
along deserted streets where the only other people
were a shy, smiling transvestite with glitter eyeshadow,
and a Chinese man clopping haphazardly down the street
on stilts, shouting *Happy, happy, happy!* over and over.

But then again, maybe I have it all wrong. Brillat-Savarin,
the gourmet, once said, *Truth only exists in the first bite,*
so maybe it was all nothing more than *perception*, reshaped
by time, desire, language, and whimsy—a *simulacra*
of soft-shell crab, eucalyptus, a pretty transvestite, stilts,
and the echoing, insistent cries of *Happy, happy, happy!*

Or maybe it isn't even simulacra so much as it's
evolution, or distillation—like the systematic decay
of radio waves, or light from a star in another galaxy,
radiating away and away, like ripples in a pond—so that,
in the end, I have to ask myself which is more real . . .
the bit of wave that splashes across my toe on the shore,

or the original, distant, and ultimately unknowable source?
Was it your voice crackling on the line from static, a bad
connection, telling me on the phone you were exhausted
by all the coming and going, or was it the dizzying intake
of breath, the instinctive inhalation, smelling each other,
in that hair's-breadth moment before our first kiss?

Days later, unable to sleep on the red-eye home, I opened
an old fortune cookie forgotten in my carry-on. It read,
The desire for space travel is a metaphor for escape,
and I wondered what it was, exactly, I wished to escape:
Perhaps the circular, rubber-band pressures of gravity
and orbit? Quotidian drone of flossing and taking out trash?
Or what about the obsessive, shark-like circle and churn
of my own thoughts, which even the glossy onyx serenity
of space travel wouldn't be able to smooth into silence?

And isn't it possible that rocket science is somewhat
overrated? All that preposterous skyward catapulting
just to quaver precariously in the quiet of the cosmos
and chug stalwartly along—space capsule reduced
to a primitive speck of protozoa. And what does
primitive *mean*, really? What to make of the terrible
purity of jellyfish, for example? No bones or brains,
eyes or ears. Certainly no heart. Just translucence,
the flimsy negligee of its astonished body a shimmering
round "oh" flushing the synovial fluid of the ocean
through itself—a pellucid scrim of phlegm hanging
in the balance between antonyms, delicate ampersand
between positive and negative, yes and no.

Or what about the underrated luster of silverfish?
Like a ruptured spray of sparks from a welder's torch,
they scatter from light, scuttling deep into cracks
and crevices, where they can remain sequestered

an entire year without food—too slippery and quick
to catch. Once I briefly touched one—cool soft body
liquid, ephemeral as mercury. It wriggled free, marked
me with a faint pearled dusting of scales spangling
the tip of my finger like the powdered glide of frosted
eyeshadow. Was this the same way you and I marked
one another? Secretly, and under cover of night?

(How soft, your flushed cheek brushing against mine,
your silvery wetness gleaming crushed pearls against
my fingers—evoking the whispered, clandestine pre-dawn
comings and goings of Heian courtiers behind rice-paper
screens, a game of smoke and mirrors, leaving only traces
of perfumed incense limning silk kimono sleeves,
a calligraphied "morning after" poem arriving by courier.)

And isn't it strange to think silverfish fossils date back
390 million years? Instinctive survivors, they'll eat holes
through these very words—disrupting syntax, reshaping
meaning—yet they never evolve, and remain incapable
of metamorphosis, shy of light, intolerant of scrutiny.
Wingless anachronisms, do they ever wish they could fly?

New Year's Eve slipped into Near Year's Day, the fortune
cookie stale but I ate it anyway, and the plane began
its descent—guided down by flashing tower lights, blinking
semaphore of flares, glow-in-the-dark strips illuminating
the runway. It seemed the plane was a clattering metal
insect, the airport a hot neoned flower—cars tiny dark mites
furiously inching along below in regimented swarms. I thought
of how insects can see ultraviolet, and how some flowers
have petals tattooed with ultraviolet-reflecting *honey guides*
to beacon the insects down into sweetness and gluttony.

Two hours and two state lines home from the airport.
I knew you wouldn't be there waiting—one leg flung
outside the covers, sleep-tousled, the porch light on
and bedroom door ajar. It was cold and clear, an infinity
of night broken only by glinting studs of stars piercing
an expansive sky. Suddenly, two brontosaurs loomed up
on the side of the deserted Nebraska interstate: life-size,
garnished in gold Christmas twinkle lights, slender necks
entwined, a red heart emblazoned above their heads.
They were corny and improbable, oblivious to the fact
of their own extinction. Tell me . . . how, exactly,
should I have read these signs, if they even *were* signs?

Things That Leave an Aching Feeling Inside

The flittering plop of moths bumping up
against the ceiling
late at night, and the shadowed, mosaic out-

lines of their bodies
littering the ceiling light's bright glass bowl—
round, triangular

wings filtering gold-hot light like tiny
black-singed hearts. I think
of the one tangled in my hair the day

before, a buzzing blur,
how it rested in the palm of my hand—
using a foreleg

to pull down one delicately slender
antenna and clean
it with rhythmic, sweeping strokes. The breathy

rush of wind during
late November storms, specked with flecks of sleet,
making the trees roll

and heave and sigh against a queasy sky
where an orange moon
wobbles in and out of the clouds, greasy

and slick as egg yolk.
Returning from the airport to empty
rooms, it makes me think

of the lover who always came to meet
me right at the gate,
and stopped on the way home for drive-thru tacos.

The razor-quick slit
of stunned clarity, so sharp I can't tell
how deep it's sliced,

when I finally admit to myself
that I've fallen out
of love. Knowing there is a part of me

that quietly waits for
this cut—for the piercing sting of silver,
for the red salty

tug of relief to bloom in warm, tulip-
bright aureolas, like
watching the wilted body of my red-

capped oranda twirl
like a twisting shimmer of silk scrap caught
in a wind funnel

when I flush it down the toilet. A cat
who mourns another
cat—whose name in Japanese meant *cloud*—

spending the entire
day obsessively searching for him room
by room. So much falls

away—our skins slipping off our shoulders
to coat our houses
in a fine layer of dust, while dust-mites

expectantly stand
in wait, ravenous to consume our past,
the selves we have lost

and continue to lose along the way,
until all we have
is what we have left to inventory:

There are moths to sweep
up off the floor, bookshelves to dust. There was
a woman who did

not know how to let go, and finally
there was the silvered
merciful flash of the veterinarian's

needle. Now there is
a cat who plaintively wanders the house
and will not eat. There

is a woman sitting in silent rooms
who is eating drive-
thru tacos by herself, listening to

the soft ticking of
the clock, like a metronome marking time
without the music.

3

when weeks

of rain

have awakened

wistfulness

Snow Country

Sometimes wet heavy snow delicately
breads the trees in coarse, white batter—
quick-dipped and flash-frozen into brittle
delicious twigs of tempura. Other days
shaking down powdery soft as flour hand-
cranked from an aluminum sifter—churning
beneath the rubbery waffle press of boots,
roiling black spin of tires, until it balls up
into the gritty, pea-like consistency
of pie dough after the flour's been cut
with silver-bladed crescents of shortening.
And sometimes, before spring, icy rain
trickles down like a drizzle of cold honey,
separating snow into crackly thin sheets
of ice, flaky as phyllo pastry in baklava,
giving way in thaw to shells of footprints
that freeze at night, fossilizing the history
of a prior day's intent. *Yuki Onna*, she is
the chilly spirit of the snow, she sings to me
in the wind, and she shifts, transforms, re-
invents herself with each fall—fracturing
and breaking above me, filtering down
slantwise from gray woolen tufts of clouds,
blanketing me with her cool white body.
I will dream beneath her, furled tight
as a Crepe Suzette sprinkled with a silky
dusting of powdered sugar until I wake to
another wet spring—the stiletto percussive
rapping of a woodpecker like the insistent
drill of mallets trilling against wood blocks;
to thunder and rain, the writhing muscular
pulse of earthworms, their labia-colored

bodies ribboned with a single blood-red band
of color, their bobbing pale and vulnerably
questioning heads; to the furred heft
of a bumblebee repeatedly hurling itself deep
into the dark purple heart of a tiny white
pansy, which topples down and flops
to the ground each time from the striped
weight of the bee. I wake alone,
and can't even begin to know what
to make of myself—raw, unsheathed
and lost in the absence of snow.

Things That Cause a Feeling of Chagrin

Thinking that because it's after midnight
one can sneak out to

the Hy-Vee for artichokes and Yoplait
without bothering

to put on a bra—wearing worn-out plaid
flannel pajama

bottoms one claims can pass as leisure pants
but realizes,

in saner moments, do not pass at all
for such—and being

deluded enough to think that surely
one won't run into

any of one's senior colleagues or former
students, thus causing

deep chagrin. When one has cooked a dinner
for a crush-worthy

woman whom one is hoping to seduce,
one definitely feels

chagrined when one's cat jumps into her lap
and promptly begins

to eat off her plate—in particular,
plucking out with dis-

concertingly greedy and delicate
precision all of

the plumpest and choicest morsels of meat
from the shrimp Creole.

Not to mention when one is pulled over
by an officer

of the law late at night on the way home
from a rendezvous

for turning right on a no-turn red light
and, when one is asked

to step out of the vehicle, finds that
one's bra is dangling

wantonly out of a sweater pocket.
And as if this isn't

bad enough, one starts to get a little
turned on, sitting in

the close proximity of the cruiser,
by the shiny badge,

jingling handcuffs and exceedingly crisp
shirt of the female

officer—it's not one's fault, after all,
that the TV show

Cagney & Lacey was popular when
one happened to be

at an impressionable age—so that
one starts to answer

the police woman's questions strangely, as if
one had perhaps been

drinking a bit (which, it should be stated,
just for the record,

one *hadn't*), thus causing things to go downhill
very rapidly

from there on out. And though one later makes
a big joke of it

to one's friends, saying one was pulled over
for D.W.B.—

Driving Without Bra—one nevertheless
experiences

profound chagrin over the incident
for several weeks.

Or then there was the time, having become
loquacious with too

many martinis at a conference,
one soon found oneself

carrying on rather *wildly* about
how one coveted,

beyond describable comprehension,
a taxidermied

armadillo to keep in one's office—
going so far as

even confessing to having priced them
at length on eBay.

Or the four months last spring when one dated
a Sidewalk Screamer,

whose favored venue for fights was one's front
sidewalk, upon which

she yelled things like, *You've just been using me
for sex!* Warm weather,

and one had no trouble envisioning
one's neighbors turning

down their TV sets to get a better
bead on it, calling

over their spouses with glee—*Dear, the dykes
are at it again!*

And as if it were the made-for-TV
movie of the week,

dimming lights and opening up their blinds—
big, buttery bowls

of hot popcorn (zapped on the fly during
silent, resentment-

filled pauses—Orville Redenbacher, per-
haps) brimming over

like squeaky, greasy styrofoam into
their unabashed laps.

Cecropia

To even try to describe the terrible voltage of
those pheromones—emitted in pulses
plagiarizing the human heartbeat's blank iambic

a few hours before dawn—would be to fully understand
raw need, desire's soft dank underbelly.
To think of it as merely *perfume* would be too pretty—

a dilution, like using the word *droplet* when one meant
ocean, or saying *could* when one meant *must*.
(Though sometimes I think perfume is all about just this *lack*—

a faint Xerox, simulated mimicking of silk moth
courtship practices, Calvin Klein models
thin puppets in a shadow play—because isn't desire

what we *desire* to desire most of all?) Just imagine
how stunted our senses are when compared
to the male cecropia moth, who can feel the scented

calling of female cecropias from over a mile
away, who if smell were sight and puffs of
pheromones smoke signals, could pick out a teaspoon of dye

randomly dropped in the vast expanse of the Grand Canyon.
His antennae *hear* the scent like drumbeats,
like the hot siren glitz of electricity sizzling

the nervous system awake until the body is transformed
into an incandescent singing hum
that flies alight, weightless without the burden of too much

thinking. The cecropias are hatching outside tonight.
They awaken, stir, and unfurl themselves
into the mild dark air through loose valves in their tough cocoons.

Painstakingly, they inflate damp crumpled wings into taut
bright kites tattooed in rich burgundies, browns,
decorative scallops, eyespots, and red thumbnail crescents.

In the dark, they find each other. Velvet bodies grapple,
nocturnal and strange, but very gentle.
Once, I lived in rooms with light switches to nowhere. Sometimes

I turned them on and off at night to see if anyone
would answer: shouts of surprised annoyance
from the neighbors, maybe a soft knocking at my window.

Once, I spent an entire summer sleeping with my front door
unlocked, convinced that through sheer force of will,
I could make him recognize this silent keening, and come.

Wistful Things

Rain-drenched heads of peonies salaam all
the way down to

the ground, broad-planed leaves sequined by fractured
glinting bits of

rain that spill off one by one all morning
as the foliage

slowly turns its green palms upward to track
the simmering

path of the sun. Underneath, the ribbed husk
a cicada

left behind, translucent, filled with water
from the gaping

hole, like a wide-mouthed Mason jar, through which
a singing winged

thing plotted the violent trajectory
of its escape.

The flash of a ladybug's wing twinkles
against asphalt

like an orange Jolly Rancher candy
and all day long

my left ovary fizzes, sizzles, burns—
a radio-

active Alka Seltzer. Ambivalence
is my longest

and most familiar companion, and we
wait together

for the small consolations darkness brings—
ephemeral

semaphore of fireflies sparking brief gold
moments into

the night, ambered shellac of cockroaches
gleaming dull red

in moonlight as they scuttle mindlessly
back and forth, cloud

of tiny insects exploding against
the brilliant heat

of a street lamp. How courageous they are.
How bravely they

blaze into ash in the bright yellow heart
of their desire

all night long while I go inside and wash
my hair with your

shampoo, purchased with the surreptitious
discretion of

an alcoholic, so that when morning's
bright blade slices

open my sleep, at least there will still be
the scent of your

hair, like ripe sunburnt apples, infusing
my cool pillow.

Bioluminescence

1. Candela

The eggs burn softly
in the earth, and when glow worms
hatch out, ravenous,

each one comes with a tiny
bright square of light like

the view-hole to a
furnace notched in its belly.
Can you feel their heat?

Their hunger for the tender
moonstruck flesh of slugs and snails?

2. Lambert

Sometimes at night, fire-
flies are startled by lightning,
the tympani-drum flutter

of thunder rumbling the storm
home, and they all flash at once

in surprise—a quick
blinking open of sleepy
green nocturnal eyes,

a phosphorescent murmur:
Go back to sleep. It's just rain.

3. Lumen

How vulnerable
we would all be if longing
shone through our bodies,

if our skins were translucent
lanterns flushed with yellow flame

leaping in the strange
and unpredictable winds
of our desire, like

the neon Morse code fireflies
use to brazenly flick the night.

4. Luciferin

You are a dusky
angel drawn to the gleaming
beam of my porch light,

a brief embered orange blaze
from your cigarette, sizzle

of sparks splattering
the asphalt of my sidewalk.
Your touch like sooty

moth wings, and I glow, suffused
with your heat, your scent, your light.

Marvelous Things

A hairy caterpillar, silvery-
plumed like a Persian
cat's tail, inching along in the ivy

on pudgy, suction-
cup feet, with eyes like glassy black pinheads.
A perfectly ripe

white-flesh nectarine one slices into
four cold sweet sections
and eats standing over the kitchen sink—

pit-stained flesh breaking
easily from the seed, juice running down
the chin and dribbling

into the webby clefts of one's fingers.
A mayfly, just at
the moment of splitting open the seam

of its former shell
and pulling itself free from its old skin,
steps into one's hand—

freshly oiled golden and brown scales gleaming
like the patterns in
a Navajo blanket—so that the first

thing its feet will touch
at the moment of its transformation
is one's skin. Brubeck's

"Blue Rondo à la Turk" in the morning
with peppermint tea.
The scree of insect song scrimshawed into

the night's horizon:
the cicadas' sandy rhythmic shaking
like cocktail shakers

and maracas; the katydids scratching
salsa on wooden
cabasas; and the short sharp whistle spurts

of crickets, also
sometimes like the soft jingling of sleigh bells.
A pair of rabbits

that come loping down one's sidewalk in moon-
light after midnight.
The owlet moth who lands on one's finger—

a merest nudge of
velvety thorax above the knuckle-
bone to adorn one

like an exquisitely coppersmithed ring—
colored like bright new
pennies decorated with shimmery

flecks of beaten gold
and maroon circles stamped in the center
of each powdered wing.

Baby garter snakes in a tangled heap
drowsily sunning
themselves in the front garden—their braided

bodies thin as shoe-
laces, intertwined in an intricate
knot work. One by one,

they disentangle
themselves, with a fluttering of red tongues,
and slip liquidly

beneath the porch steps. Raw honey, waxy
gold and honeycombed,
stirred in spooned dollops into peach green tea,

then there's a tickle
and buzz at one's lip, the discovery
of the tiniest

of bees, with miniature bands of striping,
a translucent fury
of wings. Reanimated by steam heat

and boiling water,
awakened from sweetness, and even though
it seems almost too

incredible to be true, it shakes off
the damp from its wings
and flies away into a whole new life—

miles from the petty
tyrannies of the apiary, and free
to suckle flowers.

4

in the time
of restless
nights and
insect song

Ukiyo: The Floating World

Listen. There's a spider stamping on my
ceiling with bent,

spindly legs, staccato of eight nervous
feet pin-pricking

rhythms into plaster, while its shadow
clings at a slight

diagonal, bulbous and serene, mute
as a black pearl.

Look. At dusk, the pink dwarf tulips lining
the border of

my neighbor's garden become rice-paper
lanterns—pollen-

tipped stamens flaming sulphurous matchsticks
of light inside.

A bright red dot of a bug, minuscule,
inches across

the sidewalk. I wonder if this is how
my red Jeep must

have looked from the window of an airplane—
like blood beading

up from the scalpel slice of I-80
on my way home.

I gathered up a splash of butterflies
caught in the skirl

of wind and splayed in a collage across
the metal fret-

work of my radiator grille: question
marks, hop merchants,

checkerspots and clouded sulphurs. Black-specked
fritillaries,

Pawnee skippers, and a shy butterfly
known as dog face.

Tortoise shells too, with their pinking-shear frilled
wings, and the one

I love the best—plain and moth-like,
dusted in soot

and a beautiful name—dreamy dusk wing.
This floating world's

the only one I truly understand
and I'll never

escape its slipstream—this world of shadows,
motion frozen,

and exquisitely strange myopias;
this floating world

where I coast at last into town at dawn,
all the stoplights

blinking in rhythmic yellow unison,
so I drive by

your house and flicker my headlights, although
I know you're not

awake for this blinkered gold confession
in the language

of cuttlefish, who seduce and spellbind
one another

by rippling coded patterns of color
and light through their

chromatophores. In this world I dream I'm
still in motion

when I finally drift, road-weary, to
uneasy sleep,

and where I dream of you taking the long
slim bud of an

amaryllis into your mouth, feel your
warm breath, soft tongue

licking apart the tight folds of petals,
and where I wake

the next day to the out-of-season pot,
a ruptured blaze

of red amaryllis blooms, unfurling
their dormant hearts.

Things I Would Do for You

Let me gather together a radiant cache
of jewel beetles for you—lapis lazuli blue
speckled with red and white; shimmering
green hammer-plated with yellow metal;
dapper copper pinstriping; a softly polished
celadon like glowing, apple-green jade; blue-
green lacquer lipsticked with an opalescent
hot-pink swirl; and the ones that seem cast
in the lush, buttery luster of 24-carat gold.
I will string them together with small, bright
seeds and make a necklace to warm your skin
like a dapple of sunlight burnishing your chest.

I will hand-raise mantises—feed them cater-
pillars, crickets, butterflies and bumblebees,
keep them heated, mist twice daily to make moist
fog, jungled steam—so I can bring you a bouquet
which, from a distance, will look like a glamorous
arrangement of rare blooms. But come closer,
and you will see quizzically swiveling heads,
black pinpricked eyes, sway of antennae—
perhaps the yellow flower mantid's fussy rustling
of rosebud-yellow wings notched in maroon;
or the spiny flower mantid's pink intricate frills
and spikes, violet eyes, and giant spiraled eye-
spot on leafy wings. Maybe the devil's flower
will raise its delicate bisque thorns and stripes
to you; and, of course, there will be the upcurled,
lavender-striped body, pointed cone-shaped eyes,
and pink-petaled legs of the Malaysian orchid.

I could find a Yucatan makech beetle, with
a thick and waxy back that can be carved
with an awl. I will carefully pierce the elytra
with tiny holes and notches, then set the wing
cases with gems—peridot, topaz, amethyst
and rhodolite—so you may keep it as a pet
on a sterling-silver chain pinned to your lapel.
It will toss out razor-bright prisms in slivered,
rainbowed shards of color, a jewel-crusted
living brooch clutching the promontory of your
collarbone, mesmerized by the powerful swish,
pump, and fuzz of your heart keeping time
below like a jazz bass-line, thickly vibrating,
humming and strumming deep inside your chest.

I will make you a feast of wasps, flash-fried
in sesame—oil lacquering satin-banded bodies,
glazing iridescent wings—tumble them in sweet
crumbles of brown sugar and soy sauce, served
over steaming white rice. I could garnish
the plate with a ring of crisply vigilant, deep-
fried cicadas—art deco wings spread open
as if ready to take flight—spritzed with a light
spray of ponzu sauce, for something crunchy
and nutty to nibble on. I will search through
mulberry groves for plump silk-worm pupae
to stir-fry into *sangi* for you—carefully
slicing out the midgut, tossing them in the wok
with hot oil until they sizzle. Naturally salty,
so no seasonings necessary—creamy, slick
and decadent with fat, soft and chewy like large,
ripe figs. Or perhaps, if you would rather,
I would capture dragonflies—boil them with

ginger, garlic, chili pepper, onions, and coconut
milk, serve them with an herbed coconut soup
drizzled with red ant eggs, like caviar. As an
appetizer, a dozen large and rare forest-dwelling
bumblebees, steamed with kaffir, lime leaf,
shallots, and in lieu of dessert wine, afterwards,
I could offer you live ants fattened with peach
nectar. They taste like almonds and honey.

And when it's night, I'll find a Jamaican click
beetle, also known as "Cucujo," and hold it up
to your book like a small flashlight, so you can
read by the bioluminescent spots on its thorax,
and when you're finished, I'll toss it into the air
so we can watch it zoom around the room
like a shooting star. I will draw you a hot bath,
pour steaming ladles of clover-steeped royal jelly
over your shoulders, then call in a flock
of striped blue crow butterflies to dust you
with their yellow tail brushes—gauzing your skin
with a light shivering of scented scales, like
perfumed talcum. And for music, I'll assemble
an orchestra to perform for you: first, a female
oak brush cricket, who drums in syncopated
rhythms on leaves at night with her elaborately
ornate feet; cicadas with their tymbals,
which they ripple like thunderous metal sheets;
an assortment of male moths clattering
the castanets built into their wings; for violins,
the stridulation of crickets; and finally, a water
boatman, who makes music with his penis,
as if it were a flute. Together, they'll unspool
their seductive nocturnes to beguile and ease
you into the dark velvety creases of sleep.

I know that I am strange, and poor, and prone
to daydreams, melancholy, and compulsions—
that all I have to offer are these crumpled balls
of paper scattered across my desk, these words
obsessively embroidered together with insects
used as sequins, beads, twinkly bits of decoration.
But perhaps in the silky gray light of dusk,
they might look something like the nuptial gifts
of balloon flies, with their live tiny spiders
and aphids wrapped in intricately woven, iridescent
skeins of silk—white, shimmering balloons
tightly clutched in the feet of the flies, sparkling
enticingly in the half-light like a paparazzi
of minuscule flashbulbs exploding in the dusk
during their aerial mating dances. Perhaps
you might be moved to pick one up and unwrap it,
and while you were busy with crackling paper,
smoothing out wrinkles, and reading, I might
quietly come up behind you, stroke the small
of your back, slide my arms around your waist
and hold you, my mouth in the nape of your neck.

Utsuroi

Morning light sifts
through the window
later, more tentatively.
It takes its time pooling
and accumulating
in hot buttery squares
on the floor where
the cats love to dip
and roll themselves
as if they were succulent
pieces of lobster.
Night comes shuttering
down more quickly.
The band of light that wraps
around each day like
a wide bright ribbon
is shrinking—the way
a favorite shirt shrinks
in the dryer, leaving
the day's wrists and hips
uncovered. A red-headed
woodpecker runs up
then down a wooden column
on my front porch
with splayed agile feet.
Periodically, it stops
to tap—head a thrumming
shiny blur like a sewing
machine bobbin. The cats
nudge the curtains aside
with their heads, and stare.
In the evening, lacy insects

with bodies the color
of green apples quiver
around the windows—
a shiver of filigree, drawn
to the light inside. Things
quicken. The geraniums
and dahlias burn their colors
into the air more brightly,
birds hurry in harried,
twittering conferences
and I think reckless thoughts.
Things quicken. Why
do I always love the light
the most only at
the moment of its leaving?

Temporary Things

The electric, pulsating see-saw wheeze
of cicadas

calling back and forth to each other, tree
to tree, the song

passed around from first one tree to the next
in circular

patterns—one cycle seeming to ignite
another, like

jazz musicians trading fours. Glinting
sprezzaturas

of fireflies are flashes of sequins sewn
in arabesques

on a black dress, first capturing the light
and holding it

in, like a sharp catch of breath at the throat,
then a sudden

exhalation of tiny stars. Damp musk
of grainy silt,

the river's soft repetitive licking
against the banks,

moon a ripe tangelo, and finally
the fireworks come—

ruptured sky, sizzle of rent fabric, smoke
leaving after-

images like pearled, cloudy nebulas.
And afterwards,

you and I, we will ignite, pulse, and bloom
all through the night

like rare and glamorous orchids—drawn in
first one, and then

the other, to hunger among scalloped
purple petals,

warm honey, like hypnotized bees deceived
by vanilla

and spice and musk into confusing bee
love with flowers.

And maybe, like flowers, we must seduce
pleasure the way

butterflies are seduced into stopping
for one moment

to grip the round hips of buds and uncurl
their tongues to drink.

Maybe pleasure isn't even really
pleasure unless

it's evanescent—like ephemeral
chrysanthemums

opening over the water to hang
for one moment

before drizzling down the smooth ceramic
of the dark sky

like a bright dribbling of pottery glaze . . .
egg's raw, gold yolk.

Chambered Nautilus

Today, the movers come

to empty out my rooms.
They take away boxes

and furniture, holding them
aloft—like leaf-cutter ants
transporting deconstructed

fragments of tree leaves, fragrant pink
curls of flower petals, back home
to their nest for cultivation
in mossy compost gardens filled

with edible fungus. Keys returned,
the last apartment cleaned and sealed shut,
the new apartment is a puzzle
I reassemble—from old scrap parts,
the accumulated detritus

from all my past selves—into something that's
new and hopeful, that denies the defects,
or at least disguises them as being
something else, that takes the worn familiar
tiles and, like the turning transformation
of a kaleidoscope, clicks them all back

into place in some type of arbitrary
mosaic. If I'm lucky, as in *Howard's End,*
my belongings fit like fingers in a glove
and I can pretend this transient chamber's home,
but if not, I pretend I'm on a downward
spiral toward genteel squalor in a series
of rented Paris rooms, like a character

in a Jean Rhys novel, where even squalor seems
to hold a tired kind of glamour wedged, as it is,
within a dream-like cycle of sex and absinthe.
It's a kind of compulsion, this constant moving
every few years, leaving behind old apartments
like abandoned shells when they start to grate or chafe
from being filled with too many secrets—secrets
that rub themselves raw up against the walls, scraping

off the paint and spackle, clogging up the old plumbing,
and making the ceiling buckle in a headachy
spider's web of fractures and cracks. When a structure seems
unsafe I condemn it, seal it, lock it, and move on
through a rote progression of increasingly larger
chambers until the architecture becomes too top-
heavy, and the empty chambers must be flushed and filled
with hot air, blown through a straw-like siphuncle, in order
for the entire operation to remain upright

and afloat. Sometimes I think it's all a metaphor for
memory: its unwieldy, constructed carapaces
of history and nostalgia lined with pearl. Other times,
looking out the wider operculum of a new front
window, I think it's all a fantasy of space travel,
even though I'm never really sure where, exactly,
I think I'm going—although the cold, dark, and quiet deep
preferred by the shy and enigmatic nautilus is,
I suppose, an inner if not an outer space. What do
they see down there with their primitive lens-less eyes—making

their images through tricks of light like old, pinhole cameras?
Do they see the coelacanth and recognize a stranger
from their past—chambers rewinding, pinwheeling backwards into
prehistory like reel-to-reel tapes clattering on their spools?
Do they even really see at *all*? I take my glasses off,

look out from my new front window onto the unfamiliar
street below and feel the blur: camera obscura, velvet
photographer's cape, wooden box steeped in sepia after-
images like a tea-stained cup that holds the tint and flavor
of past leaves. I wonder if what the nautilus sees is right-
side up or upside down. Who's to decide the difference?

And what can possibly ever come of all this tiresome spiraling?

Things That Are Filled with Grace

A centipede, waddling across one's floor,
striped like fruit-stripe gum
with elegant tail wisps trailing behind—

perfected fluid
marching of leg after regimented
leg like the rippling

synchronicity of a pianist
practicing Czerny
exercises up and down the keyboard.

The giant holly-
hocks that begin the day like round, *café-
au-lait* bowls, with hand-

drawn lipstick-pink petals on the bottom
and warm, sticky-sweet
honeyed centers. They open themselves up

into dinner plates
by noon with a precisely engineered
choreography

of unfolding, the way collapsible
metal vegetable
steamers unfold themselves. A grasshopper

that flings itself up
out of a patch of clover in measured
cadences, with bright

flashes of marigold-yellow under-
wing, and a shower
of castanet-like clicking raining into

the air. A giant
hulk of a beetle, clinging to the string
of my porch light like

an overweight P.E. student hanging
on gym ropes, who then,
improbably, begins to maneuver

itself with clever
dexterous footwork upside down and right-
side up, then upside

down again—deftly plying the twirling
string with the practiced
muscular grace of a *Cirque du Soleil*

gymnast. The tiny
pale green nymphs that mistake my bedside lamp
for the moon, swirling

in clusters within the warm gold halo
of light, then pausing
to rest for a moment on the opened

pages of my book
like uneasily shifting hieroglyphs
that cast strange shadows,

causing me to misread things. And after all,
isn't it really
just such a delicate smidgin of life

that separates *love*
from *leave*, *fear* from *feat*, *spectacular*
from *testicular*,

and *grace* from *grief*? How is it that starfish
are each perfected
in their architectural proportions

to form the ratio
of the Golden Section? Why do the leaves
of the artichoke

map the same mathematical sequence
as pinecones, daisies,
seed heads, and cauliflower; and who tells

snails or the chambered
nautilus to initiate the in-
finite, spiraling

logorhythms of the Fibonacci
series? How do bees
know which egg to select for their new queen,

nurse bees ladling
royal jelly over the larva once
she hatches, sealing

shut the royal chamber with wafers spun
from wax and silk? They
let her slumber for seven days before

she's reawakened:
a lambent, ambered, incandescent bride
and queen, obsessed by

a hard-wired and fearless desire to throw
herself at the sun—
fierce and elusive in her skyward flight.